Tribe, Caregiving LGBTQ and Straight Ally Friends

Michael Boyajian

Jera Studios Publishing

Tribe, Caregiving LGBTQ and Straight Ally Friends

Michael Boyajian

Copyright © 2025 Michael Boyajian

ISBN Hardcover: 9798377281658

ISBN Paperback: 9798377281498

Library of Congress Control Number: 2023903421

Jera Studios Publishing

Fishkill, New York

Dedicated to my late wife Jeri and all the members of Tribe, or any other Tribe.

Author Page

Contents

Introduction 7
1 Case Studies 9
Images 101
2 Conclusion 129
About the Author 139

This book has no chapters per se dividing the story even between bad times and thanks to Tribe good times because life is not linear it is circular as perceived accurately by the Native Americans best seen in the book by Hyemeyohsts Storm, Seven Arrows.

Introduction

"We have too many high-sounding words, and too few actions that correspond with them." - Abigail Adams letter to John Adams, 1774 (Not enough people helping one another Tribe style is what this means today)

Those that perpetrate hatred often profit from that hatred." – Michael Boyajian, 2023

What is Tribe, the one I belong to? Well, it is all women LGBTQ and Straight Allies but for me. The only male and affectionately nicknamed by Tribe as Token

Dude. Whereas Abigail Adams is appropriate again at this point:

"Remember the ladies," -Abigail Adams writing to John Adams at the onset of the Continental Convention March 31, 1776.

John Adams as well as the other all male delegates did not heed Abigail Adams but 247 years later Tribe heeds it in reverse by remembering the guys, one actually, me Token Dude. Enough said with this mix of seriousness and levity as to the glass ceiling which will give way, or is giving way, just as did the once impenetrable fortress walls of Constantinople. Believe me, to paraphrase Grace Slick at Woodstock in 1969, a new dawn is about to arrive America.

1 Case Studies

We will learn how a group of LGBTQ and straight allies compose a group of friends they call Tribe whereas members look after one another as a benevolent society offering help of any kind whether it be a midnight call from someone in emotional distress or the need for a pet sitter because of an unexpected emergency hospitalization or even just socializing at barbecues, game nights, minor league baseball games or seasonal celebrations. Helping others does of course extend to those outside the group as well. It is perhaps a lifestyle model that much of the rest of our society has forgotten to follow and perhaps now after reading of the Tribe will return to because it really does in the words of former Secretary of State Hillary Clinton takes a village or if you will Tribe.

My friend Sal observed an aged group of gays who take turns making dinner for one another

My friend Anna had heart problems and we take turns driving her to treatment.

Me in the hospital writing this on the eve of surgery and Tribe cares for my pets.

BEGINNINGS

My late wife Jeri flies around and around me filled with mirth if I need cheering up. She is a witch (Wiccan) and crossed the rainbow bridge to the other world and comes back over to this side to be with me and I with her more often than not and it is more common than you think a fact verified by my doctors (scientists) who say we are just now on the cusp of understanding this other world (see, Hello from Heaven) and what I know is that the door between the two worlds are wide open and will never ever be closed again sort of like a door providing entry and egress to an enclosed garden like the Beatrix Farrand garden at the FDR Library grounds.

She departed this world separated from me at the end by Covid restrictions leaving us without closure but at the wake luncheon in our friends Jody and Jeanne's backyard Jeri appeared as a shaking bush that only I could see and only I knew from its mannerisms that were Jers mannerisms when excited crying out to me look I am here we are still together and continue to be so with her presence growing stronger and stronger.

And although she is a higher being knowing all she still has feelings and can still have them hurt as do all those from the other world and she visits with her sister Stacey and niece Jancie and nephew Derek and other family members quite frequently

And others visit me now although you have to keep your eyes open often to see a sign from them like when I get the dropsies like my dad Harry used to have always dropping things so when I do that it means he is visiting and letting me know he like Jeri is by my side and sometimes it is another known person of late for the dropsies the famed Arab traveler and writer Ibn Battutah, who went further than anyone prior to steam power including Marco Polo and who Jeri turned me onto with gift of a fine edition of his book.

And Jeri's mom Marilyn and dad Gus have appeared to let the family know Jeri was ok and with them across the rainbow bridge and I tell everyone now who has lost a loved to keep a careful look out for the first sign of them visiting from the other world until they grow stronger with live so mow Jeri has morphed from different appearance and actions even holding my arm while we drive together through the country side.

And she likes to relax in a photo of her taken at her favorite restaurant Pandorica in Beacon New York the Dr Who restaurant with our favorite recent Dr Who and companion turned Dr Who over her shoulder and it's an enchanted photo with her Mono Lisa like expressions sometimes hard to read like today when she showed no expression as I searched for Halloween movies for us to watch until I realized yesterday was all we needed in the way of Halloween movies watching the Ghost and Mrs. Muir and Bell Book and Candle both of which in some respects resemble our current relationship though not entirely on point but close enough for a heavy heart.

So, this is not another book I have written about Jeri but a book about the other world and the rainbow bridge and her Coven called Tribe which is a benevolence group helping each other and others in need while celebrating nature.

Let's begin with my comment on the human rights of witches in today's New York Times (October 29, 2023) a little past the anniversary of her passing September 14, 2020 and almost upon our favorite holiday Halloween but please don't think we don't love Christmas or the holiday season in general. Let's begin.

My New York Times comment has commented on the human rights of witches.

My late wife was a witch ("Wiccan") and her coven was called Tribe and acted as a benevolence group helping out members and others during times of need and they were in tune with nature around which their celebrations were based. As a former New York State human rights judge I can say with absolute certainty that witches are recognized by the United States government providing them with burial rights for military service at national cemeteries and allowing their symbol, the pentagram, to be displayed on their headstones. They have been persecuted for thousands of years mostly drawn out from misogynistic hatred and were the first group in America to be targeted for hate crimes best seen at the Witch trial memorial in Salem, Mass.

Carry on, as the Hillary Clinton supporters like ourselves like to say...

What to do when the leader of Tribe is stricken? Others of course rise to the occasion and put their shoulders into the work at hand moving like a vast ant army. So it was when Jody was rushed to ER at 2am for what turned to out to be a cardiac emergency requiring a stent but leaving her quite weak so that her maximum endurance was to walk back and forth up and down her two car driveway. Weak but glad to be alive. Her partner Jeanne and son took command and were by her side the entire time while communicating Jody updates fell to Latina extraordinaire Roxy who performed marvelously like a NASA press secretary leading up to a successful lunar mission landing back on Earth. I wanted to order a shipment of Katz's Deli from New York's lower east side but thought it not a good diet idea for someone in her state of recovery so

I put in a short order for myself (lol) and ordered a massive gift basket of dried fruit and nuts for Jody and also recommended she as I had once done in recovery walk the Dutchess rail trail to get her endurance back using the succession of memorial benches as milestones. Back and forth to the first bench then eventually the second bench so forth and so on until you were up to a mile and increasing your speed and so good to go just like that a snap.

The cancer whisperer. That's me a good thing to help friends or family battling the Big C as John Wayne used to say but emotionally tough on me knowing they faced certain death.

My dad Harry had pancreatic cancer a hopeless diagnosis back in the 1980s as it is mostly today but for my personal hero President Jimmy Carter who dodged that bullet that felled every other member of his family and the humane president was studied to ascertain why he was spared of all the others and to learn if there was the possibility of a cure, though the problem with pancreatic cancer is it was hard to detect and once it was it was detected at that stage it was unstoppable. Oddly enough the host for the TV show Jeopardy looked pretty good right up to the end while my dad was a huge hulking man reduced to someone akin to an Auschwitz concentration camp Holocaust victim.

Conversation was a bit tricky you had to avoid talk about something upbeat in the future which might sadden them because they most likely would not be going or getting to see it happen.

Then there was Jeri telling me to go to Egypt without her and I firmly stated Egypt then was a permanent no go without her company because she was most of the reason for taking a trip anywhere including Egypt.

My dad who was a lifelong Yankees fan out of the Bronx who got to see Babe Ruth to Joe DiMaggio to Yogi Berra to Micky Mantle to Reggie Jackson to Dave Winfield play in, as Art Rust Jr. would say, the great ball orchard in the Bronx. For him it was a comfort to just watch Yankee games with me. He always said in fact he didn't care who won as long as it was a close game.

My brother in law Bob was into concerts he had seen and Phillies baseball where as an artist he sketched caricatures for fans at the home games. His concerts went back to the 1960s to the present. Jimi Hendrix to the Stones. So those were the subjects for conversation.

Joel was a late 1970s New York City politico and he ran in the Democratic mayoral primary campaign during the city's financial crisis facing off against incumbent 104th Mayor Abe Beame, Ed Koch, Mario Cuomo, and Herman Badillo. And then our time when I worked for him on a computer graphics magazine where every day there was a technology revolution. And also, his live broadcast each week from his company's upstate radio station bashing Soviets during the Cold War and not letting Russians take copies of our technology magazines at trade shows because President Reagan said no high tech information access to them. But I couldn't talk to him about my exciting future legal career.

My mom's second husband Haig who was battling colon cancer shared a hospice room with a young kid who blasted heavy metal music from a giant boom box during hospice and you couldn't ask the kid to turn it down because it was his way of coping with the certainty of death and besides Haig was in so much pain he didn't even hear the music. We would just talk about the art of business networking. Haig was a retired manager from the Harvard Coop and a retired adjunct professor also. He loved to take my mom out sailing and schmoozing it up at political fundraisers for the Kennedy family. I flew up to Boston almost every week to help out.

Getting back to my brother in law Bob who wasted from lung cancer sitting bed side with him in hospice with his arm moving upward in slow motion during morphine drip for ten minutes unsure where his arm was going turned out to itch his nose and then he became lucid for an instant and turned to me and said, Hello Mike, before going back into the fog.

Fred a Mainer and Old Brooklynite who was the editor of Walt Whitman's newspaper The Brooklyn Eagle. Swapping old political stories was ok as he deteriorated from jaw cancer.

My best friend in the Hudson Valley, Tom with cancer everywhere just sitting with him each day listening to his music collection playing on his $10,000 digital stereo designed with a near analog audio sound. Autobahn to More Hot Rocks to Tubular Bells to Quadrophenia.

All these simple acts made not only my sick friends and family like Tom's wife Kathy happy and the same with Joel's wife and my sister in law Stacey too.

Jeri had 9-11 induced stage four metastatic breast cancer that was dormant for 19 years that she beat and was recovering until we got Covid prior to a vaccine and cure whereas she was gone in two weeks without me by her side because of Covid restrictions. My role was more like her marathon coach and pin cushion where a hug would do wonders. For years I mistakenly thought she left mad at me until I found a lost voice mail to the contrary that I missed from her and she wasn't mad at all and well she came back from the other world across the rainbow bridge anyway to be with me and that was a real ok thing to happen.

Buddhism's realization of the unborn awareness of the mind needing compassion first before awareness occurred and not a lot a little will do. For me it was in elementary school hosting backyard Jerry Lewis muscular dystrophy carnivals to raise money for the cause. We're talking 15 to 30 bucks but that qualified enough for compassion purposes in Buddhism. Also, another act of compassion was in junior high was pet sitting the special ed kids' pet bird. Actually, this was more fun than working with a singing bird in my room and the wonderful touching thank you letters from the kids. Same with the carnivals building a puppet theater out of a washing machines cardboard box and putting on puppet shows with puppets made out of old socks and other performances and games that also made the neighborhood kids happy.

Later my wife Jeri and I would put on Buddhist puppet shows on social media using real puppets and a puppet theater that were so cheeseball and silly but really cracked up the Tibetan Buddhist lamas (monks) and rinpoches (high level monks) who watched the shows.

My late wife Jeri's social media friend Christina the owner of a top London bookstore reported that she is a recovering alcoholic who hit bottom in a state close to death but was able to detox herself and with the help of AA and friends survived Yes she is alive today serving the world with her very popular independent bookstore and because she was helped by what amounted to her own Tribe and she is also helping others to and on the road of recovery posting for instance how to reach recovery services with a few taps on your device and also posting a Pink video titled Sober and if you have been there and lived it will bring you to tears. Back in the 1980s people knocked me because I detested a popular TV show that depicted a incorrect view of life in a bar as something glamorous almost as if a bar was a Tribe but bars were sanctuaries from violent hate decades ago for the LGBTQ community but your average neighborhood pub was not and as you descended in a trajectory down to Dante's Inferno expecting someone special was going to walk through the door that never happened and either you did what Christina did and detox or you died and it didn't matter that you had your own seat at the bar. The Navaho and other Native Americans know this fact and that the Native American genome proves that these beautiful spiritual people have a strong genetic propensity to alcoholism and so on the two nations my late wife Jeri and I visited, the Hopi and Navaho, alcohol is outlawed to save what remains of the once massive population that spanned two continents and was reduced by ninety percent by invasion, disease and alcohol. And that is why if you bring so much as a can of beer into the Navaho or Hopi nations it's bye bye for you and a direct ticket to incarceration. Think. Check out the Pink video which is a Tribe and that London book shop is Treadwell's.

I myself have careened into the abyss when a friend committed suicide. I stopped going to class, broke up with my girlfriend, stopped eating properly and drank and drank and dropped out of college and it didn't get better until I met my late wife Jeri who also had issues but when we joined together it was like two atoms coming together to form precious molecular water, H2O, whereas when all was said and done Jeri had an illustrious career at the Met and became a noted artist while I became a Court Street attorney helping people in need and became a judge where with Jeri in mind and the Yoda like training by my county leader Arthur and political friends like Sal I was offered a choice, help the rich and powerful and move up the judicial food chain or help those in need. I chose the latter, virtue, viewing my judicial appointment as an opportunity to be compassionate and help people as do most government workers. And boy did I help a lot of people while serving three governors. I was judicial Tribe along with thousands of other government employees. Yes. Not bureaucrats but truly compassionate beings.

The breakthrough book 1619 by Nikole Hannah-Jones and the New York Times is in itself Tribe, offering catharsis to African Americans for the violent hatred perpetrated against them for centuries in America where even peaceful spokespeople were killed from Martin Luther King, Jr. to Malcolm X to Medgar Evers. By the way I regularly get threats particularly a crazy who plays a buzz saw into the phone and my doctor says to back off the political statements in public because it is bad for my mental health and I may be putting my life in jeopardy. However, in the words of F. Scott Fitzgerald, so we beat on, boats against the current...

No longer was that horror hidden or denied and as an Armenian that was for my people the most maddening thing, the denial of our genocide with reparations being inconsequential to the trauma and denial of the catastrophe and as my father always said, if it did not happen then where are all my uncles.

And for African Americans the lie that slaves were treated compassionately or that slavery would end on its own are themselves complete fabrications. If you want to see how slaves were really treated read Frederick Douglass, 1619 or look at the Civil War photograph of the slave Oliver Gordon the so called Whipped Peter photographed by McPherson and Oliver whose entire back was shredded by whip welts. this was one but of many like images taken by various photographers that were part of a special exhibition at the Met a few years ago. These photographers and slave victims were also Tribe showing the world with their own eyes the sadistic treatment of slaves.

The President of the Confederacy himself, Jefferson Davis, stated the plan was to push slavery to the Pacific Ocean and then expand south to the very tip of South America creating a vast slave empire. So that despite ongoing contemporary travesties against Africans by rouge police, 1619 offers some catharsis by making Americans aware of this up to now secret history. The book onto itself is Tribe.

So too is Tribe is President Joe Biden's acknowledgement of the Armenian genocide with its 1.5 million slaughtered after 106 years after that catastrophe and my Turkish friends that acknowledgement had no adverse impact on Turkey as feared by them in fact the instant the earthquake hit

Turkey and Syria I immediately sent money to a rescue organization on the ground there and my two Turkish students from back in 2009 when after retirement as a judge I taught at Fordham that summer both remain friends on social media and one of my favorite authors is the Turkish literary giant Orhan Pamuk who wrote Snow and Istanbul among other titles.

And Pamuk under threat of death has stood up and acknowledged the Genocide making him in my opinion worthy if inclusion in Profiles in Courage by President John F Kennedy a book that every person of my dad Harry's Greatest Generation had on their bookcase even if it was the only book on that shelf.

And of course, the greatest tool of Tribe turns out to be your smart device carried by billions of people worldwide allowing for ease of photographic or video documentation of hate crimes in real time and with ease and a few taps on the device viral broadcast of such travesties worldwide.

Billie Holiday. Strange Fruit

If you won't believe your eyes believe your ears by listening to this jazz song that if it doesn't frighten you with the idea of lynching victims, human beings, as non-sentient hanging fruit than you really should seek help and I don't mean that rhetorically.

It was announced today, February 18, 2023 by the Carter Center that President Jimmy Carter had chosen to go into home hospice rather than continue with further medical treatment. Did you know that as President he laid the groundwork for energy policy that we use to this day. He could also have summoned all the powers of the greatest superpower in history to attack Iran but then the hostages would all be dead, and who would know better than he a naval officer and a gentleman. Did you know that Rosalyn had meltdown when he said they were leaving military service to go back to the peanut farm in Plains, GA to go into politics. Did you know he quickly won the governor's race in Georgia and then the presidency of the United States. Did you know after his term of office he pulled his farm out of multimillion dollar debt. Did you know that both he and First Lady Roslyn took an active role in the Carter Center she as a mental health advocate and he as a worldwide election monitor and environmental advocate and all else eradicating so many horrible, deadly diseases in Africa and protecting elections at home as well as abroad. President Carter wasn't just a tribe member but instead exemplified the center of a Tribe, My Captain, My Captain, we salute you. Holiday Tribe

I was very active with the Brooklyn Republicans back in the 1990s. The Brooklyn Republican leadership was led by a very wise African American gentleman, Arthur, and 80 percent of the leadership was African American or Caribbean American and a little known fact was that this liberal organization held great sway over the statewide party because the county had more

Republicans than any county in the state and because of the county's strong liberal bend they were able to put Republicans in the governorship three times and in the mayoral seat five times despite the 5 to 2 advantage of Democrats over Republicans.

The mother elephant protects the baby elephant figurine given to me when I got Very active with the YRs and LGBTQ Republicans. Sal is Tribe leader and above him Jason. If I was getting a little hot with rhetoric Jason would pass a below the radar time out to Sal to give to me when went I back to the Democratic Party. That's how the parties used to work, opposite sides but able and necessary to work together and we will, I am confident return to that model.

Just think when you got to vote and your check in table has two usually senior citizens working at the table one Republican and one Democratic who were a very long day for a little pin money to have lunch with their friend. They view this service as a civic duty not an ideological battle or get rich scheme they are there out of a sense of duty and these two workers spend most of the day chit chatting cordially with one another when they have down time from checking in voters they are the fundamental political building blocks, the foundation if you will, of our two party political system.

Anyhow along the way I was put in charge of the Republican holiday party which was attended by elected officials (for instance congresspersons or judges) from both sides of the aisle all coming together for seasonal cheer putting politics aside.

One of our leaders, Eddie, asked me if he could play the holiday tunes at the party. He reminded me of me whereas all I wanted to do was play my vast collection of holiday songs over Christmas Eve and Day but my family and Jeri's both said no. Why, I don't know? So, because of that I had empathy for Eddie and so appointed him as our official holiday DJ.

And year in and year out Eddie would sit alone on the stage playing holiday music as happy as could be through his CD Walkman plugged into the sound system from the beginning of the party to the end.

Well one day we leaders were appointing delegates and alternates to the 2000 Republican Convention.

I was an alternate in the 10th congressional district which was entirely ceremonial and Arthur and his co leader Madge were actual delegates along with Eddie in the 10th. Suddenly Eddie stood up and said he didn't want to do it again and left whereas without hesitation our chair Arthur swung around and said Mike you're in and so began my Cinderella rise to the upper echelons of the GOP. Leaving it all at that, the job propelled me into a state judgeship serving ultimately under three governors —Pataki, Patterson, and Spitzer whereas I saved live music on Broadway and unionized 100,000 children care workers under Governor Spitzer's instruction making me one of the top judges in the state. This was Tribe.

This was especially true knowing that two more groups were to come before me to gain representation through, as did the child care workers, a new union voting method called card check where you just simply counted cards filled out by workers and if representation was attained they could begin earning living wages and those were farm workers and domestic workers.

I interviewed an author named Alondra Nelson for a radio segment I once did for my friend Chris's Stony Brook University Radio. She had written a book about the Black Panthers entitled Body and Soul: The Black Panther and the Fight Against Medical Discrimination.

Contrary to white perception of the Black Panthers as a militant African American organization Nelson points out that they were a nonviolent group dedicated to providing social justice to Africans Americans in the form of healthcare establishing a large network of free medical clinics and healthcare educational services all in an effort to battle medical care discrimination against that community a trend that studies even today hold as true and still ongoing.

The Panthers carried out this mission from 1966 to 1980 and most likely broke ground in the need for healthcare reform which decades later was met in part by the strides made by Obamacare. Nonetheless, based on the above mentioned statistics more work is needed in the area of healthcare delivery to minority community.

The Panthers medical philosophy might even have led to being recognized by environmentalists as having an adverse impact on the community caused by members of the community clustering around dangerous environmental hazards giving birth to a new environmental movement known today as Environmental Justice which also seeks to battle medical discrimination caused by minority population exposure to hazardous sites.

Therefore, the Black Panthers were Tribe as is author Alondra Nelson for reporting the true story of the Panthers as a healthcare provider as well as the scientists who broke ground with the establishment of Environmental Justice through demographic studies.

We can go a step further to former Secretary of State Hillary Clinton and her unwavering belief that it takes a village to not just raise children but adults as well leading to her greatest achievement as a U.S. Senator that being the groundbreaking parity law that mandated that insurers provide equal coverage to those suffering mental health illnesses as is afforded to those suffering physical ailments. That law saved many lives including my own which my late wife Jeri personally thanked Hillary Clinton for when she and our friend Anna met her at a book signing at Oblong Books in Rhinebeck after also relaying her gratitude earlier that year when Jeri met Chelsea Clinton at a women's event in the Hudson Valley region guaranteeing Hillary Clinton a place in the highest realm of Tribe legacy while she at the same time destigmatized mental illness which in itself saved countless lives of those who often self-medicated with alcohol and drug abuse a futile effort at treatment.

Speaking of me and Jeri's friend Anna we for years would have season tickets to the local minor league ball club, the Renegades, who were at that time a Rays franchise but after Jeri passed they were taken over by the Yankees organization which would be ok with being Yankee fans but more into the game itself so no longer into the rivalry thing like Jeri and I loved Boston so why are we going to hate Boston over a game and the same with the Mets because we are all New Yorkers after all and also Baltimore is a party town with a great ballpark so we liked the Orioles, especially their uniforms and logo of the Baltimore Oriole which by the way if you that bird in Baltimore and your with Baltimore people they will deny it's an Oriole and it's just a Robin.

We don't argue it's some kind if custom there involving the bird. Trust me Jeri and I were members of New York City Audubon for many years and know our birds and have a lifetime list around 100 birds some even from overseas which we got into the habit of looking out for after reading that President Jimmy Carter and First Lady Roselynn did on all their overseas trips.

As for Anna, she is a diehard Mets fan and probably had a meltdown when she got the news about the dreaded Yankees taking over her minor league club. As for the Mets the rivalries were more friendly than hostile I mean we kids loved the Boston players like Yaz and whether you were a Mets or Yankees fan everyone was cheering on the 1969 Mets and every kid to this day can name every player on the 1969 rooster one of whom is our Baltimore Orioles friend Bob's cousin Ron Swoboda famous for the winning amazing diving catch which he recently wrote a book about called Here's the Catch.

And the rivalry between the Mets and Yanks was so friendly to the point there was annual charity game between the two teams called the Mayor's Trophy Game. By the way is paid to do Tribe type benevolence work, she is a government therapist working with veterans suffering from PTSD. And of course she is LGBTQI+ and was having discrimination problems with and I successfully guided her through that as an attorney and former human rights judge to an amicable conclusion, gratis of course, or as the legal profession calls it, pro bono Latin for without charge, with the Tribe member discount.

And of course Anna being a practicing Buddhist on the Dharma Path picked up some good karma from her work helping veterans and when she needed help getting back and forth from the hospital because of a heart condition the entire Tribe took turns taking her to and from the hospital without complaint for a year until her good health returned.

As for Ron Swoboda I asked for a photo of him in a Yankee uniform a team he joined after the Mets he didn't have a meltdown over the request but made it known that in his heart he was and always would be a 1969 Mets World series champion player Any request I made through Bob for myself or friends and family starting with the aforementioned Yankee uniform request came with a big heart and written inside was, 1969 Mets.

The pros are really ok even when retired when one day on Yankees Old Timers Day Whitey Ford came off the crosstown shuttle subway to change to the uptown subway to Yankee Stadium and everyone was kidding him if he knew how to get up to the stadium giving him a good laugh.

Another time I was walking to my office in the morning from Penn Station and almost got clipped by a speeding car making the turn though I had the walk sign and I glared at the car and it was Yankee coach Bob Lemon who looked back at me with a grin pointing to the crosswalk sign which by now said Don't Walk which gave us both a big laugh and I am sure at that hour he was rolling out of the famous nearby bar Toots Shur popular with all the local professional Athletes.

There was also superstar Reggie Jackson playing along with the fans who would throw coins on the field after each game because he was the original "money player" and he would stay out there until he picked up every last coin to the satisfaction of the fans, his fans.

I was once in a beach town pub on Long Island where at that time many Jets football players lived and on my way to the restroom the doorway became completely filled with what seemed a giant, it was Jets superstar part of the so called Sack Exchange, Joe Klecko. He was nice enough to spend time talking to me and I remembered they were playing the nemeses Miami Dolphins, prior to the arrival of ultimate nemesis Tom Brady and the Patriots years later, and I like a nanny told Klecko he better not stay out too late with the big game tomorrow. With that he laughed and said ok coach and strolled away with a chuckle.

Other tales incuded Phil Rizzuto at a trade show a story about Rick Cerone, Uncle Gary and a Joe Namath story. Dallas Cowboy auto accident deposition. Billy Martin getting razzed at Fenway and looking at me for help. Pete Rose at Gracie Mansion for Mickey Mantle organ donor night a Tribe thing for him to do. Lawrence Taylor unknown to me behind me at the car rental line how could I miss while all my co workers were going ga ga. Joe Pepitone busting my balls for an autograph on high holy day at Yankee Stadium Opening Day.

Sa'sl 5 old gay friends taking turns cooking dinner just to have company.

One must also consider Pope Francis as Tribe for with a wave of the hand ending the false narratives of the so called culture wars and its participation in by 1 billion Catholics with perhaps even impacting those of other faiths implicitly declaring the ludicrous belief in a war on Christmas a complete fiction especially in light of the fact that the holiday season accounted for retail sales of $960 billion in American dollars in 2022 up from $416 billion in 2002 meaning if there really were a war on Christmas it failed miserably.   No holiday season no economy and therefore no prosperity.

And Tibetan Buddhist Tribe leader, His Holiness the Fourteenth Dalai Lama has called prosperity beneficial to precious human existence for all equally a few years ago at the start of a four-day retreat at a sold-out Radio City Music Hall. And as for those who are critical of the slow pace of change in the church, please realize it is impossible to change things on the dime with a diverse global flock of 1 billion people but bear in mind change is inevitable.

My sister-in-law Stacey on Long Island and neighbor Ann here in the Hudson Valley are both Tribe for their devoted, heroic and compassionate efforts at caring for often ignored cat colonies in their respective locales and for bringing many into the comfort and safe sanctuary of their homes with colony care not just being an American trait but global in nature where Jeri and I saw such caring people at work with colonies from the Alhambra in Spain and at the foot of the Acropolis in Athens itself. It is time we realize that cats, dogs and other animals are sentient beings with certain rights a position supported by many legal scholars today and based on the scientific findings of botanists worldwide that trees and other non-domesticated flora are also sentient beings.

And this issue is being evaluated spiritually by many sects of Buddhists today where once the belief was segregated to the confines of Zen Buddhists alone. The proof lies in the scientific evidence that trees for instance communicate with one another not like humans but in their own way and remarkably will transfer nutrients to a sick tree and even a tree stump. It is worth noting that domesticated flora as found on farms are not sentient probably due to centuries of agricultural breeding. So, let's recognize all these beings as Tribe. On a final note a tip of the hat to Ann for not only caring for cat colonies but for single handedly banning the circus from this county because of the inhumane living conditions of circus animals where Ann stood alone 24-7 in front of the circus entrance here in all types of weather conditions until they were shown the door. Tribe.

Tribe. George Washington. Viewed spy network as the fun part of job. He was popular and Martha even more so the original power couple. He was hand picked for command by none other than John Adams who was impressed by his uniform which Washington had custom made designed to impress and his cv in the

French and Indian war. As the war wound down a mutiny was gaining ground at the Catonement near Newburgh where many troops were stationed. In his usual style that rivaled the status of rock stars he stood before the throngs in the hall known as the Temple of Virtue. He pulled a pair of eyeglasses from his pocket which in those days was viewed as a great disability. He placed his glasses on his face and said, I have grown old in the service of my country. He brought the house down with many soldiers reduced to tears. The closest I think we've come to this was Steve Jobs standing before a who's job who of computer executives and saying I am Steve Jobs and I was fired from Apple bringing the house down.

Tribe for World. Delian League, Roman Empire, Allies, NATO, NAFTA, EU, Commonwealth, Pacific Rim

Who is Tribe

Jody, retired RN

Jeanne, retired RN

Anna, therapist

Jennifer, professor

Roxy

Dawn

Kim

Late wife Jeri, Artist, Met librarian

Me, Mike, Token Dude, former state judge

Marriage Equality NY Tribe

Cathy

Michael

Robert

Brian

Ron

Rob

Me, Mike, Straight Ally

Preservationist FSD Tribe

Mara

She got a preservation story in the Newb York Times

and 1000 front covers worldwide

LGBTQ political Tribe

Sal

Dave

Rick

WORK TRIBE. There was another kind of Tribe and that was for a kid to find a job when there were no jobs in the late 70s. Shine dads shoes. Sell Christmas cards. Newsday route in mall hide competitors cart. No tips. Vic turns it into a mega operation. Selling Daily News subscriptions. Temp agency screwing in one screw into a thousand boiler parts until all had a blister on our palm which we would hold up as a greeting sci fi like. Temp job at clothing factory all had Hobbit paperback in the back pocket of our jeans. African Americans kids as hungry for work as whites Bread man at supermarket. Moving thousands of trees. 1000s of chicken parts. Gym worker. Landscapers. leaving USA for work in Valencia. India. ESL teacher online with Taiwan corporation teaching students in China Japan South Korea and Taiwan. ESL at Fordham University French Russia Taiwan Italy China Spain Brazil all happy. Beyond book publisher. corporate executive lawyer judge.

The UNESCO World Heritage Site and Catholic Tribe of Notre Dame after the catastrophic 2019 fire that destroyed a great deal of Notre Dame Cathedral in Paris Catholic and non Catholic jumped into action to save grand spiritual site. Many including Jeri and I launched social media fundraising campaigns dedicated to the Cathedral. We were just starting to really pull in donations when suddenly the wealthy donor class got swept up by the groundswell to rebuild the World Heritage Site pouring millions of dollars into the effort whereas we smaller operations fell idol with most people seeing no need to donate in light of the big bucks crowd opening up a massive cash flow spigot. Hey but that didn't mean we small donors were forgotten. Quite to the contrary our early efforts were greatly appreciated and acknowledged by Michel Picaud, the president of Friends of Notre-Dame de Paris a leader of the restoration effort and by high up church luminaries around the world including His Eminence, Timothy Michael Cardinal Dolan here in the U.S. who along with Michel Picaud went out of their way to reach out to all who took part in the restoration no matter what level of contribution was made and to provide detailed regular updates as the restrictions progress. The cathedral is a classic example of French Gothic architecture built in Medieval times over an ancient Roman temple on the Ile de la Cite in the Seine River. The cathedral is expected to reopen in the Spring of 2024. It is of course well known as the setting of the Victor Hugo classic novel The Hunchback of Notre Dame and has appeared in many films based on the novel. This restoration effort is one of the finest examples of the entire world locking arms to preserve not just a French cultural treasure but a worldwide cultural treasure. God is truly great.

Union Tribe. Because of this Tribe you no longer hear the Dickensonian cry, are there no work houses. As my dad said when we were kids debating around the kitchen table, you can say whatever you want around this table but don't bad mouth the Unions, they put food on the table and give us our health care; and no guns.

9-11 Tribe

On the promenade we all look at one another what to do. Go to Brooklyn Bridge workers crossing over covered in white dust saying never going back. Houses of worship have tables chairs and water set up. Go home wait for Jeri. She arrives just says going back between bridges only 20 years later do i realize what she went through military jets. Sirens. First responders. Fumes. She gets home and we do count of who we know who worked at WTC No one. Phone rings. Bruce started there 2 weeks ago come to Long Island for a family meeting. Jury duty and anniversary still Bruce goes in. Plane right after he hung up with Irene. We are asked to go in and look for him We agree. Blood bank lines but no Ned blood realized something terrible had happened. We go in smells of dead. MTA says it was a Chinese buffet gone bad. Mayor's office helps take swab from Jeri give squad car no luck and cop can't go to NJ put up pictures go to cantor suite after four days give up. After some time they find a piece of Bruce with dna we support efforts to revive lower Manhattan Patti smith Sheryl crow David Johansson etc. bring people to ground zero. 19 years later Jeri had 9-11 cancer beats it but get Covid and gone in two weeks. Contact with other side long road back. Every one unified. Bush on rubble with firemen.

YOUR HOME IS TRIBE, The Fortress

don't walk away from it fight like hell to keep it. Design and maintenance. Library garden decor cooking entertainment art creating (Jeri was art and I books and articles) politics local and Hillary. I do watercolors Love. Painting. Investment. Spend and value goes up. Home protects it's a guardian.

1841. Apothecary. Ghost. Jeri presence. Ancestral furniture. We eat cake for breakfast in this home History of home and property originated with Van Wyck and neighbor Glenn ancestors on the list of dead. Try to connect to Underground Railroad because of hidden attic and rough hewn wood. Fishkill supply depot beams support basement ceiling Underground

Railroad was so secretive that need a Quaker connection to prove

Antique bottles and windows

ANTIQUE GLASS IN ROMAN OR ARCH OR EVEN GOTHIC STYLE OF (the window style as described in the 1926 book by Stephen Rensselaer titled Early American Bottles and Flasks) WINDOWS IN MY HOUSE DATED 1841. In addition to the large collection of antique glass bottles the living room window glass panes of the house are also antique and all intact but for the right window's lower right pane which had to be replaced with modern glass due to a lengthening crack in the antique glass. The trademark blur of historic window glass is best seen in different light, time of day or weather conditions. Today was overcast about mid afternoon and the antique blur is best seen in the right window with the one contemporary replacement pane and remaining three antique panes (to the right of which is the home's bronze historic plaque as a key to which window I'm talking about) whereas you can see the blur in the reflection off the glass panes that are antique whereas in stark contrast the replacement pane's reflection is crystal clear or without blur. But for that view the signature antique glass was nearly undistinguished. The Peabody Essex Museum in Salem on their historic home tour the guides report early glass windows as being a sign of affluence of the nation with say one of the so called witch houses being near Medieval with very small windows, and a few years later larger windows are in use providing better viewscapes and more entry light into the home whereas by the time of my house being built in 1841 it was the affluent period for antique glass as can be seen by the very large two living room windows in my saltbox house. The antique bottles and windows I believe are all within the 1800s with many tied to the apothecary who lived here and had a shop on Main Street here in the Village of Fishkill as indicated by a perfume bottle label in the collection. It is my understanding that all the bottles and window panes were blown in much the same way as often demonstrated by the craft people at the Hudson Beach Glass gallery and demonstration studio on Main Street in Beacon in a renovated ice house in operation since 1987. The bottle collection from my home has representations of all types from tinctures to perfume to medicine to alcoholic beverages etc. Following my windows are some from the historic homes of the Peabody Essex Museum and then some Hudson Beach Glass cats.

Cleaning bottles

Beginning to clean the antique bottles found on property. Can clean about 80 percent of them. Have first half in sink filled with warm water and denture powder for overnight soaking and will brush and rinse out in morning and start second half cleaning. Let's see what happens.

Family tree moon landing Gus was here at home and an American Revolution ancestor was at fsd who served at depot.

Where would I be today if my dad hadn't given me a book as a child titled Tell me Why. It just about answered any question a kid might have about the world around us and it sparked something called curiosity. Then my uncle Gary rolled in with a regular supply of books starting with a 1908 Ed of Jack London's White Fang and a book on Ghengis Kahn and then a Western cavalry genre titled Boots and Saddles and my mother in law also got me into Westerns with Louis Lamore and Tony Hillerman and of course my late wife Jeri got me hooked on ancient history by giving me a book about Sumer by Woolly. My brother Vic helping me through the pitfalls of choosing a law school and then getting through that first year which gave birth to books and films like Paper Chase and One L sending first year students into paranoid fits of panic but at Brooklyn Law School our dean at the time Judge Trager at orientation said look to you left look to your right one of you won't be here but he said if that were true none of you would be here. That was the big line from the law professor in Paper Chase. Then one of the senior profess professors stated Brooklyn Law

School was known for producing judges I chuckled at that thinking that will be the day if I ever became a judge well sure enough I became a state judge Dean Trager became a Federal District judge and many of my friends became judges. What about Jeri turning me onto ancient history. Well, my first judicial appointment was as a human rights judge and then the states labor judge and then an unemployment judge during the financial crisis and ended back at human rights supervising a team of investigators clearing out old cases all of which time I served three governors. But the point I am making is Jeri turned me onto ancient history when I was a Court Street attorney and then in 2000 I became a human rights judge and then fast forward to today April 3 2023 and I'm still reading ancient history and three years after Jeri passed I'm reading her category ancient Near East history books and her favorite ancient book Gilgamesh which brought me to tears and inside Jeri's mind and how close we were like the protagonist in that first book in history and then I come across the Persian King Cyrus and I learned that in the 6th century BC he established the first human rights declaration in human history that I ordered a replica of from a dealer in Canada that is called the Cyrus Cylinder and so the Persians did a lot more than fight the Greeks having cylinder which I ordered so there is a little loop through some family Tribe (the cylinder was created by Persian king Cyrus after he conquered the oppressive Babylon regime.

The cylinder ordered the return of forcibly displaced of people who were moved by Babylon back to their homelands, interpreted to without doubt to include the return of Jews to their homeland, reparation of the god or gods to the wronged people of different backgrounds forced into the Babylon empire, and declared Cyrus as a benevolent ruler who rebuilt the destroyed cities and culture of the oppressed peoples by Babylon.

And by the way the Persians called themselves Iranians from the beginning of their 9th century BC appearance on Earth and that the word Persian was a misnomer though not out of disrespect given the Persians, Iranians, by the Greeks not unlike our reference of the people of Byzantium as Byzantines when in fact they considered themselves rightly as Romans (of the Eastern branch of the Empire differing from the earlier branch as being of Christian faith as opposed to the pagan pantheon of gods dominating the West until it too went into the Christian domain) who contrary to the British historian Edward Gibbon in his 1776 (interestingly a year that marked the creation date of what would eventually become the greatest superpower in history, the United States of America the leader of the Free World) book The History of the Decline and Fall of The Roman Empire actually were not in decline but repeatedly expanding and contracting in size over an additional one thousand years following the decline of the traditional Western Romans who themselves logged in a thousand years going from republic to imperial rule until the agreed termination of the Western empire dated as of 476 when the Emperor Romulus Augustulus (ironically the name of the mythological founder of Rome Romulus and then the name of the creator of the all-powerful

Imperial Rome, Augustus) was overrun by Germanic tribes followed by the collapse of the Byzantines or the Eastern Roman empire in 1453 AD just a few years shy of the 1492 discovery in the words of Europeans describing the trans-Atlantic indigenous peoples of what Europeans called North and South America.

And Byzantium didn't just run out of energy but were overrun by unrelenting Ottoman Turks who breached the thought to be impenetrable walls of the Byzantine capital, Constantinople, using a new technological advancement gun powder invented in China and effectively used by the Turks to power a new military weaponry innovation, artillery, that blew away those once impenetrable walls of that city. So, a city that was once founded as Byzantium and then changed by

Roman emperor Constantine to Constantinople and with the Turkish takeover became Istanbul as it was known as throughout its subsequent history right up to today

I could go on talking about my sister Dee's husband Tom who helped care for my dad in the later years of his battle with pancreatic cancer where I couldn't be there as much as I wanted because of major problems at work that led me to law school with the provision from Jeri that we move to the city so she could jump start her art career which worked with her becoming a noted New York artist showing in Chelsea SoHo the Village the Hudson Valley and Europe. And my sister-in-law Stacey talking with me to 4 in the morning as I tried to deal with the loss if Jeri as well as my family and a few friends like Bill and Hanna. My life didn't begin until I met Jeri and hers did not begin till she met me and when I asked her why did you pick me? She said you were interesting.

My mom and brother helping us to save our home with financial help that allowed us to successfully weather the financial crisis of 2008 that occurred just when I lost my judgeship.

My genocide scholar and social historian Uncle Gary also have interesting books like Kon Tiki and one about a TV late show predecessor to Johnny Carson Jack Parr and then when my dad Harry retired he got a part time gig in the library at Ole Westbury College and he would bring home boxes of books they didn't need all espionage books by both American and British authors all at the height of the Cold War

Me and Jeri were book people, bibliophiles. We loved visiting bookstores every weekend and in September the 6th avenue book fair followed by a Yankee game and then a September food break at the San Genaro festival in Manhattan's Little Italy.

And every Friday night we would eat out with Jeri's parents Gus and Marilyn alternating between two Mexican restaurants and then heading out to an independent movie theater for a flick. We paled around with her parents quite a bit.

And Jeri and I were really into the city before we even moved there Jeri landed at the Met and me at a nice mid-sized magazine publisher, I even did an independent study with a Professor Taylor on the literature of New York and I read every book on that all-encompassing reading list he gave me. Before the city career track I worked at a book publishing house where the owners taught me everything about publishing and the owner Rudy's advice led me to my first book Green Enchantments decades after I gave up writing back in the day to go back to college to earn my degree and everything he taught me I ended up utilizing for the 50 books I have written in recent times The art and science of book publishing has remained the same only the technology has changed.

The SUNY tribe oh yeah to hell with your private schools I could spend my life attending every school which each of its own special character in the system beyond my alma maters Buffalo State University and Stony Brook University where I met Jeri to kindred souls into books art culture punk rock and booze and eclectic dressing prior to hitting the career track. The schools like Binghamton Oneonta Brockport UB Plattsburgh Fredonia New Paltz Albany Farmingdale Old Westbury Purchase Orange Potsdam etc.

But in contradistinction: Buffalo State University Breakdown of Tribe

After my first year at Buffalo State University our best and brightest transferred out to better schools leaving the campus almost tantamount to a state of lawlessness or a place that lost its moral compass. Luckily for me I was able to get by with the help of friends along the lines of Xenophon's handful of hoplites marching out of the Persian Empire surrounded by a million hostiles until I too transferred out. Unfortunately, at my new school Stony Brook University I entered into a downward spiral averting a crash landing when I met my future wife Jeri who also averted a crash landing of her own by meeting me and together we came together as a formidable one, along the lines of - E pluribus unum - out of the many one. Whereas together we rode together to the pinnacle of our respective career ladders for me corporate executive, Brooklyn Law School Moot Court Honor Society, New York attorney and state judge and author of over 50 books and Jeri invulnerable flying below the radar hence a stellar longtime 34 year career at the Met and as a noted New York artist. In other words we lived together along the lines of Secretary Hillary Clinton's mantra, It takes a village and though we had many mentors we were together that village. Enough said.

Tribe acknowledged by first Egyptian woman Egyptologist and director of the Cairo Museum, Wafaa El Saddik, in her book Protecting Pharaoh's Treasures at page 129 at the very end of chapter 5. Among other Egyptologist she acknowledged was Met Egyptologist Dorothea Arnold.

For some reason I got it in my head to organize all of Jeri's ancient Near Eastern books which she had begun to do before she got sick. And back in the day she turned me onto those books and that got me into ancient history. Let me get to the point. Lately I have been reading a lot of books by and about Egyptologists. The last one was about the first European woman Egyptologist who was also the first woman employed by the Louvre, Christiane Desroches-Noblecour. Today I started another Egyptologist book this time by the first Egyptian woman Egyptologist and director of the Cairo Museum, Wafaa El Saddik. The book's title is Protecting Pharaoh's Treasures. The first few pages were so filled with sorrow about what happened over there it brought me to tears. And Ironically she reports it is safe for tourists now but the tourists don't believe it and so all that remains of the tourism there is just 5 percent of what it once was. Anyhow I got it in my head that maybe if she were to speak at the Met it could help to begin to turn the situation there around. I am writing you because you have a way of getting things done there best seen in Jeri's memorial service at the Met. You know how to work the levers at the Met. Let me know what you think. Mike Boyajian.

Like President Barack Obama said of Secretary of State Hillary Clinton, She did everything I had to do only backwards.

Ham radio Tribe

Check in traffic regular radio messages. Not nerd game's but emergency manages. When the grid is down we are still up.

Buddhism Tribe or Sangha if you will

Buddha Dharma Sangha

Hometown Catskills Tribe childhood to now

Southern Tribe

Reading Imani Perry's South to America you learn of the South Tribe or if you will the two halves that make up the South Tribe, White and Black still separated but in subtle ways with Whites refusing to concede African Americans as equals. Before law school I was a sales manager and traveled the country and enjoyed visiting the South which a brief time was on track to the stars based on the idea of the New South which was felled by racial and grievance politics. I also like the Southern writers who were in their own category among American writers and were both White and Black. There was a richness to the prose perhaps a sad lament. Faulkner and Toni Morrison those two alone make the South a major literary region. And I always got a kick out of William Faulkner working as a screenwriter in Hollywood who would say, let's see if we can make a story out of this Hemingway book which drove Hemingway so crazy that he would only deliver his manuscripts to the Nevada California border never entering California My southern sales manager was Walter. He was a native southerner out of North Carolina at that time living in Atlanta or as he called it Hotlanta. After a day of sales calls we sit on his veranda making great conversation while he barbecued away with his specialty being pork loin. We had breakfasts at the Waffle Houses and lunch at the home cooking places where they just kept pouring the ice teas out of endless pitchers. I don't know how I held that much ice tea. One day coming back from our

Atlanta to Alabama sales run he pulled the car over and ran out into a cotton field and brought back a sprig of actual cotton for me. I kept that cotton for along time but only recently did I understand the meaning of that cotton. Walt lives in Chicago now and like many New South believers headed North out of the South which seems to be slipping back into the ditch Neil Young once sang about which was blasted by Lenord Skynard with both sides saying it was all lighted which to this day I'm not sure about. Yeah my brain had a lag time with thing's southern and things African American until law school probably because of my being raised in very segregated Long Island. Which was a project my boss Jyll, a deputy commissioner at New York State Human Rights and I were working on at my last stint at that agency. Jyll found a book called Sweet Land of Liberty and asked me to read it and find some evidence of Long Island segregation. Well around page 90 I believe I found it with the creator of Levittown quoted as saying he would not sell to African Americans because it would scare away White homebuyers. We'll soon after that I was shown the door told my Obama funding was depleted. Jyll exited soon after. She always said you enjoyed things I was denied. True. And she wasn't shocked when I told her I spent my teenage years at Jones Beach and never saw any black person there ever. A film documentary came out around that time which showed the same black man over and over again. I even doubted that. Robert Moses the builder of Jones Beach didn't want to scare off whites either. I could go on but let me say that a young African American woman set at the next cubicle over from me in our offices and she was exited about Jesse Jackson running for president and I said but he can't win. She just shook her head kind of saying that I didn't get it. The point is as the MSNBC host Vlishee said about his dad running and losing. That wasn't the point. The point was he could run and that is the point I missed big time with that Jesse Jackson supporter. It wasn't about winning it was the fact he could run for president a glass ceiling that was broken years later by one Barack Obama. See also Beautiful Creatures the film. On a final note the author's first name Imani means faith.

And don't think this racial outrage is isolated to the south and that it wasn't just Long Island segregation or slaves were used at the popular historical site Philipsburg Manor in Sleepy Hollow where today they operate an actual slave garden or that Brooklyn itself was under voting rights act scrutiny until the Robert's court overturned it saying there was no longer discrimination in the US regardless to Birtherism and hanging president Obama in effigy in white face on the steps of the Capitol but in New York slavery was abolished in 1817 but it was grandfathered so that the last slave in New York was freed in 1827. But the real low life of all time goes to Texas for not telling the slaves that they were free for two years and only then because the Federal government was finally able to field an army big enough to head down to Texas and enforce the law.

Apartheid class at stony Brook years before anyone knew what that was about and as a judicial intern following the law clerk of justice Charles kuffner, Richard Fuchs as he worked on the definitive book that indicts General Bedford Forest as a racist who slaughtered African American soldiers while soaring white soldiers and who went on to run the KKK Soon after the publication of Richard's opus, An unerring fire, the statues of forest started coming down.

Juneteenth we first learned about attending meetings with the Southern Dutchess NAACP who by the way are not afraid to thank the FBI for helping to end discrimination against them at one time.

Systemic racism? Does it exist. Yes. Want proof. Watch the loved by everyone holiday season classic movie Holiday Inn starring Bing Crosby, Fred Astaire and many other stars both men and women and black and white. But don't watch the one on TV though. That is the edited sanitized version. Watch the DVD and I guarantee when the movie reaches the February holiday Lincoln's birthday you're sure to be shocked when Bing Crosby rolls out in black face and the African American staff sing about Lincoln being their protector white father. Even It's a Wonderful Life is flawed. As a human rights judge I spotted a number of violations especially the early scene between Jimmy Stewart's brother and their African American housekeeper and of course the condescending attitude towards Italians referred to as garlic eaters and treated by others in the cast as look how liberal we are we associate with Italians. I know these movies provided work for performers of color but.... My late wife's niece and her husband became quite wealthy and purchased an old style Victorian mansion on the water on Long Island. One day they were rummaging around the attic and they found all sorts of memorabilia about a once famous black face duo. One of them owned the house but died from alcoholism sort of like what John Lennon called Instant Karma. So what do you do when you discover that in your home's history.

Native American actors ranking on John Wayne and other white performers in their native language in very graphic terms while making westerns and cavalry movies. Native American studies at college and beyond to Navajo and Hopi nations

Lets get very serious now. The Native American population was reduced by 90 percent on two continents through European war and disease. Did Tribe fail them. Almost. But ten percent survived and so they today more than just exist, they teach all how to love and care for the Earth and all its inhabitants. Tribe did not fail.

Jeri and I were fortunate to meet a literary giant, Native American poet, author, professor, playwright, and saxophonist Joy Harjo who was the 23rd United States Poet Laureate, the first Native American so honored yet she took time out at the 2017 NEA Big Read event at the Poughkeepsie Library to write a very thoughtful note to me with her signature in my copy of her book, How We Became Human.

She wrote, "For Michael, May this inspire your own poems and stories, Joy Harjo." Joy Harjo is a member of the Mvskoke Nation. Joy Harjo was born in Oklahoma and lives in Hawaii. She has been the recipient of many other prestigious awards recognizing her creative achievements.

As part of that year's NEA Big Read Jeri and I were honored to attend a performance at Bardavon in Poughkeepsie by Navajo and Ute flutist R. Carlos Nakai in the front row directly before him and he was accompanied by the Hudson Valley Philharmonic, the late Randall Craig Fleischer conducting.

Review of Poet Warrior by Joy Harjo:

There's a reason why Native American poet, author, playwright and saxophonist Joy Harjo was the United States Poet Laureate. In this memoir she shares the sorrow and tough times that will make you say yeah

I've been there yet she will seamlessly show you the way back to the sunny side of life while teaching Native American history like but differently than the book 1619 does for African Americans. Time for a Pulitzer and a Nobel for Joy Harjo whose favorite childhood poet was Emily Dickinson who delighted her with the query "I am a nobody are you a nobody." Well Joy Harjo you aren't a nobody and because of your writing neither are your readers.

Of course Jeri and I had a special Tribe once where she and I and her mom and dad, Gus and Marilynn, would pal around together starting with dinner and a movie every Friday night and other fun things until illness struck all our lives where what remained of paling around was no longer the same but as Tribe the healthy would care for the sick until in the end there was but one left alone, me – that is if you disregard the fact that Jeri especially and her parents and many others who have crossed the rainbow bridge exist now in our world because the door between both worlds is wide open and Jeri's presence is so very strong that our Tribe together is like the film, the Ghost and Mrs. Muir.

Images

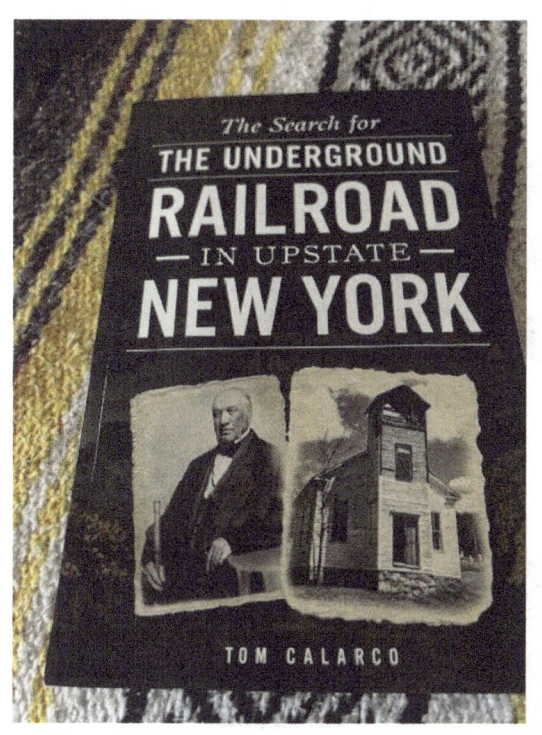

	The Stanley Kulesza Family	Joh
Kukic	The Wladyslaw Kulesza Family	Jose
and Milica Ivosevic	The Kulfan Family	Juli
	Anthony John Kulgavchuk	Mar
ybraniec Kukich	The Joseph Kulhanek Family	Jan
	Adeline Sirganian Kulhanjian	Ann
ela	John Ohannes Kulhanjian	Josep
ka	John Onnik Kulhanjian	Theo
hn Kukis	Karekin E. Kulhanjian	Frida
s Kukis	Krikor Kulhanjian	Samu
Weber Kukk	Nahabed and Aghavni Levonian	The K
Kukkola Family	Kulhanjian	Floren
ukkonen	Onnig Kulhanjian	Ladisl
a Kukla	Serpouhi Hashmanian Kulhanjian	Michal
	Yeranouhi Kulhanjian	Piotr K
Kukla Family	Lillian Kulhawy	Stanisla
kla	Eugene Kuliberda	Alexan
	Alexander Kulich	Balint K
is J. Kukla Family	Anna Pastuch Kulich	Peter N.
kla	Katherine Botoj Kulich	Paulin

Bovino	Aghavnie Boyajian	The T...
	The Bedros Boyajian Family	The B...
	The Bedros Boyajian Family	The A...
	Bertha Manougian Boyajian	Antho...
	The Boyajian Family	Arthu...
Bovio	Dikran M. Boyajian	Arthu...
L. Bovis Family	Gabriel Boyajian	The B...
Bovit	Hagop Boyajian	The B...
	The Harry Boyajian Family	Bridget
	John George Boyajian	Bridget
itz	The Kerop Boyajian Family	Brigid C...
	Krikor Kachadoor Boyajian	Catherin...
	Misak Boyajian	Catherin...
Bovolak	Munjeg Boyajian	Charles
	Nazareth P. Boyajian	Charles
water	Nishan Boyajian	Charles J...
er	Ohannes John Boyajian	Claude A...
d	Osgan M. Boyajian	Cornelius
amile		

2 Conclusion

WHERE THERE IS FAILURE OF TRIBE

Reading Imani Perry's book, South to America, it dawned on me that the fact that many of the founders were slave owners is intractable and forever taints their democratic beliefs beyond the criminal horrors of bondage to the point that their democracy, not unlike the Athenians, is further limited to those in the words of The Rolling Stones, of wealth and taste. So that is the conundrum we find ourselves in where we claim freedom for all but to this day limitations are imposed by the ruling class on all the rest of us especially the traditional democratic outcasts, African Americans. As a lawyer we are taught our job is to solve any legal problem we face. So why not apply that method here whereas in the past I explained that what happened in Salem was a witch hunt as was the similar hunts prior to that in Europe whose proponents took great pride in the extraordinarily high number of witches, mostly women, they had killed leading me to digress as to Justice Alito's rationale for overturning Roe v Wade being based on a Medieval treatise by a witch hunter and what was his personal death count of witches - hundreds or thousands or more which was the historic norm. In any event I went onto say that in modern times there are no real witch hunts but rather the adoption by political fanatics of the formula of a witch hunt which is a very successful formula for the means to an end that is genuinely evil as can be seen with the Red Scare, McCarthyism, the race card, black listing Pete Seeger and the unrelenting and unfounded barrage on Secretary Hillary Clinton permanently damaging her political aspirations. So why not take this idea of formula and apply it to the democratic principles of those who are now viewed as morally flawed where we adopt and expand these principles to everyone and throw the principles' authors under the bus. And this can be done and is not an impossibility for if they can move the massive statue of proto progressive though morally flawed President Theodore Roosevelt on horseback with it's almost invisible adornment of two obviously burdensome people of color from the entrance to to the American Museum of Natural History an institution founded by he and his family, then we can do likewise to the others without also disposing of their important words and ideas that include "we hold these truths to be self evident" or "I have grown old in the service of my country." It is a

Buddhist belief that ultimately all will eventually be gone through the impermanent nature of all things but the idea of Buddhism will always exist so too the idea of democracy though it's flawed proponents and institutions will be gone through their very own impermanence and isn't that the core nature of democracy of voting, impermanence, so that evil will eventually always be shown the door.

Whereas in 1619 the reader is infuriated with every turn of the page over the violent hate driven injustices that have been perpetrated and kept secret for far too long against African Americans, in Imani Perry's recounting of the history of human bondage in America it is told by a delicate weaving into the story of contemporary visits to the South where one finds that things may appear changed but below the surface things are much the same where no one will stop you from eating in a breakfast restaurant but once inside no one will talk to you in fact in the words of Ralph Ellison you will be invisible where only by leaving the establishment will you be able to breath freely again and that is the essence of her work, you are not infuriated as in 1619 but even worse, simply heart broken by how much has changed but remained the same in that what was once above the surface is now systemically below the surface so life for African Americans is not unlike the trees in Alaska described in The Treeline by Ben Rawlence where trees seem to be surviving despite the permafrost turning to slush above the ground caused by climate change but unfortunately below the ground at root level climate change is melting that permafrost into slush only this slush is drowning the trees causing the forest there to disappear along with its dependent human inhabitants.

I am reading a book about climate change wiping out the last great forests on our planet by Ben Rawlence entitled The Treeline and learned of an indigenous people in a dying Russian forest called the Nganasan who based on what I just read have given up on their culture and their language and their way of life and their very existence. Perhaps you can make them aware that they have certain rights under the United Nations Declaration for the Rights of Indigenous People and try and get some cultural resource support out to them. I am not seeking to challenge Russian authority it's just that as an Armenian I know after the

Genocide my people's cultural candle almost flickered out but for the fortunate support of France and the resurrection of our intellectuals in Paris in the 1920s while working creatively along side with the expats from around the world who set up what Ernest Hemingway called A Moveable Feast in the City of Light whereas Armenian culture rebounded and thrives globally today. As an aside, I was invited many years ago to take part in the inauguration of the United Nations Universal Rights for Indigenous People at the UN complex in New York. My thoughts are just a heartfelt suggestion.

Putin the basket case threat and China wandering into Middle East quicksand which will become immediately inconsequential in two years with the total roll out of electric cars globally by every car makers where even my currently advanced Toyota hybrid goes obsolete

Criminal Justice inequality beyond the death counts young teens being sent to prison to do hard time. See them going home on train and saying looking at the platform clock I'm never going to forget get that time and date.

TRIBE FAILURE CHINA

Chinas rich dynastic history went back thousands of years and seems well chronicled having its ebbs and flows but not sputtering like the Byzantine Empire but more like the theory that holds there was not one big bang but several so too the heights reached by each new Chinese dynasty but for aberration inside one where they took a giant leap backwards where the emperor recalled its massive armada of a thousand ships many dwarfing any other ship sizes at that time. The pull back was inexplicable and allowed the European sea merchants to fill the void a few decades later which spelled trouble for the Middle Kingdom until the birth of the Communist Party or if you will today's Chinese dynasty. And again there is the aberration again this time with China moving away from lucrative relations with the trillion dollar economies of America and the Freeworld to hang out with the economic basket case, Russia led by the last Soviet Putin the homicidal sadist indicted war criminal being wiped out by a lesser military power, Ukraine. It seems China is undergoing a dynastic retraction where

Mao suits and near starvation economics is the norm again. C'est la vie.

GOOD NEWS CONCLUSION

GOP says no more politics you are a judge now I make decision do I rule conservatively and move up the judicial ladder

Or do I do the right thing and with Arthur in mind I do the right thing starting with reverse discrimination case passed over by ten senior judges saving live music unionizing 100,000 childcare workers and helping the flood of unemployed during the financial crisis

About the Author

Michael Boyajian is a retired attorney and former human rights judge. He is the author of over 50 books. He lives in the Hudson Valley with his two cats where he enjoys his Cicero garden and library created by he and his late wife Jeri Wagner

Made in the USA
Monee, IL
01 May 2025